Patriot Fire Team
Equipment Guide

Paul G. Markel

Patriot Fire Team

Equipment Guide

Paul G. Markel
Copyright 2020
All Rights Reserved

Contents

Chapter 1

What is a Patriot Fire Team?

A person standing alone can be attacked and defeated, but two can stand back-to-back and conquer. Three are even better, for a triple-braided cord is not easily broken.
Ecclesiastes 4:12

Many moons ago, I became a United States Marine. During my time in the Corps, I had a few different jobs, but my primary MOS (military occupational specialty) was that of an Infantryman. When I was on active duty, the core unit of the Marine Corps Infantry was not the Company, Battalion, or Regiment, it was the Fire Team.

When I went through Basic Training and Infantry School, I learned all about the Fire Team and its composition. The basic Fire Team consisted of four men; a Team Leader, a Automatic Rifleman (who was also the Assistant TL), an Assistant Automatic Rifleman, and a basic Rifleman. The ranking seniority flowed in that order as well.

If the TL was killed or injured, the Automatic Rifleman became the leader and duties were passed down the chain. Every man was required to know how to perform the duties of the man ahead of him.

While examining the myriad natural and manmade disasters in the United States during the last few decades, one thing was clear to me; the citizens are always on their own. Whether we are discussing the aftermath of Hurricane Katrina, the numerous riots in St. Louis, or the recent media-created panic of the Corona pandemic, the criminal element of society is never deterred by a disaster and law enforcement is always spread thin.

For at least thirty years, maybe longer, the mainstream news media has painted the term "militia" in a negative light. This has been done while completely ignoring the role of the militia in the founding of the nation and the Federal Law, "The Dick Act of 1903", which formally codified and legally affirmed the Militia as a national security resource.

Much confusion abounds regarding militia or training band construction and formation, so much so that I decided to simplify the matter with the Patriot Fire Team. The PFT is simply four friends, neighbors, or like-minded individuals who have pledged to support each other and their corresponding families during times of crisis or emergency.

This is not conspiracy or paranoia. Numerous times during our nation's history we have witnessed the need for the people to protect their communities and neighborhood from riotous looters and roaming gangs of criminals. We saw this play out during the sixties and seventies; Watts, Detroit, and Trenton. We saw it in LA in the 1990's. We saw it in St. Louis and Baltimore just recently. And, of course we saw it in the south, particularly in New Orleans, after Katrina, and we will see it again. Add to this list the riots in Minneapolis and numerous other cities in 2020.

The idea that the police will always be around and available to protect the people during disasters and riots is a laughable fallacy. We have borne witness to the failure of that myth time and again.

A Patriot Fire Team is not just about security and fighting off looters, though that is one role, the PFT is there to support other members during personal trials and hardships; loss of a job, loss of a home from a fire or disaster, etc. The Patriot Fire Team is about friends and neighbors being prepared to care for each other, regardless of the origin or reason behind the troubles.

In the book, the Patriot Fire Team Manual, I detailed how to go about organizing, training, and leading a PFT. During this book, PFT Equipment Guide, we will go into great detail about the necessary equipment that every member will need and should possess in order to deal with the sudden and extreme dangers that their community may face.

As a bonus, we will consider some specialties or unique roles that members of the team might have to play during a national crisis or localized disaster. This text, combined with the original PFT Manual should provide the dedicated and concerned American citizen with the information needed to effectively prepare for the hardships that almost certainly lie ahead for the great Republic of the United States of America.

"The mission of the Marine Corps rifle squad is to locate, close with and destroy the enemy by fire and maneuver, or repel the enemy assault by fire and close combat." - USMC FMFM 6-5

Chapter 2

Personal Protective Gear

All Team Members

Primary Armor

Level 3 or 4 hard armor plates (front/rear), capable of stopping 5.56mm and 7.62x39mm rifle rounds. Designated plate carrier, preferable with MOLLE-type straps to allow pouches and carriers to be affixed. Plates can be steel, ceramic, or some other type of composite.

Alternate Armor

Level 3A (IIIA) soft armor panels with a designated carrier. (Defeats handgun and buckshot, not rifle bullets)

Primary Helmet

Level IIIA Kevlar helmet capable of stopping handgun rounds, buckshot, and fragmentation as well as some grazing rifle fire. Chin strap and helmet padding for fit and adjustment are required. Standard ballistic-type helmets include; MICH, ACH, or PASGT. The ACH and MICH helmets are more versatile than a PASGT helmet. PASGT helmets provide a bit more protection. If you see the designation "ATE" that means "above the ear" ergo, the ear area is cut out to allow for ear protection muffs and comm gear.

Alternate Helmet

Any type of hard, padded "bump guard". The bump guard helmet provides protection from traumatic impact to the head, but does not offer ballistic protection. "Bump guards" are easy to obtain; think hockey, skateboarding, rock climbing helmets. Motorcycle/ATV helmets can hinder the ability to properly aim a rifle and make it nearly impossible to get a cheek weld. Also, a motorcycle helmet can limit peripheral vision.

*Protecting the head from traumatic impact is a crucial and an often overlooked hazard. Even if looters and rioters do not have firearms, (and they likely will) the danger of thrown rocks, broken pieces of bricks and concrete, and bottles is always a threat.

**Some type of light hat or soft cover should be kept on hand for times when the helmet is not being worn. It is important to keep the sun out of the eyes and off the top of the head.

Ear (Hearing) Protection

All responsible and intelligent shooters will use ear protection as well as eye protection when they are training with firearms. In the 21st Century, our troops now go to war with ear protection in place. On a personal note, when I was a member of the 6th Marine Regiment and we breached the Iraqi minefields to invade occupied Kuwait, I had yellow foam ear plugs protecting my hearing.

We have come a long way since 1991. Electronic hearing protection muffs that filter out ear damaging sounds, while amplifying friendly sounds, are available from numerous retailers and a good set can be had for $50 to $75. If you spend the extra money, you can purchase electronic hearing protection that plugs into your handheld radios.

The primary concern with muff style ear protection is whether or not they will fit under your helmet comfortably. If you have a PASGT or MICH helmet, simply remove the ear pads on the left and right. Most bump guard style helmets already have cutouts in the ear area for muffs. A good place to start is to look for ear protection with a flat head band.

If you do not have electronic muffs or cannot afford them, at very least, all team members should have some kind of ear plugs on their person at all times. Hearing damage is permanent and preventable.

Eye Protection

Every member of the team should have both tinted and clear wraparound style eye protection. Shatter-proof eye pro is readily available everywhere firearm accessories are sold.

For those who wear prescription glasses, they should be shatter-resistant and large enough to protect your eyes. This is not the time for the old Ben Franklin spectacles. Also, regardless of the eye pro, a safety strap is a wise choice to keep them on your face during strenuous physical activity. I should not have to tell you that a tiny piece of fragmentation, sand, or dirt in your eyes can take you out of the immediate fight or hamper your ability to see a threat.

Gloves

Like your eyes, your hands must be protected. Regardless of how strong your armor might be, if your hands, particularly your dominant hand, are injured you will be of little use to yourself or your team until they are repaired and healed.

The two primary threats to your hands are cuts (slices, scrapes, and splinters) and burns. As with armor and helmets, there are various levels of hand protection. Kevlar or Nomex gloves provide protection from heat/burns as well as cuts and scrapes. However, these are more pricey than common work gloves.

The Mechanix line of gloves is probably the most popular and readily available protective gloves available in the USA. Mechanix has a variety of styles, some include impact resistant gloves with hard knuckle protection.

Regardless of the brand of gloves, the most important attribute is fit. Your gloves should fit your hand snuggly with no extra room in the fingertip area or wrist. For the PFT member, gloves are essential protective gear, not just for warmth against the chill. You must be able to accomplish all your normal tasks with the gloves on. These tasks include, but are not limited to, employing all of your weapons, rendering first aid and applying a tourniquet, using Comm. Gear and other electronics, operating a vehicle, etc.

Author's Note: While it might seem cool or "tactical" to cut away the fingers on your gloves, this is amateur folly. The whole purpose of wearing gloves is to protect your hands. If your trigger finger is lacerated, how effective will you be to your team? Rather than cut the fingers off of your gloves, actually go out and train with your gloves on. No, snipers don't need to cut the finger out of their gloves. I went through sniper school and fired every single shot with gloved hands.

"Anyone still present five minutes into a gunfight is a participant."

-MSgt. Paul Howe U.S. Army Special Forces, Detachment Delta

Clothing / Uniform

The clothing you wear should be loose enough to allow for kneeling, crawling, and sprinting if the situation calls for it. Clothing must be rugged and from a reliable manufacturer. Broken zippers and lost buttons will ruin your day. Pants and overshirts (Military Blouse) should have ample pockets for hasty storage. Ample military-grade clothing is available on the surplus market.

All Team Members should be prepared to wear the same type and color of clothing for uniformity sake and ease of recognition. Camouflage choices will be based upon the area of operation. (Teams in the east or midwest would have little need for brown desert uniforms, while those in the southwest would stand out in green woodland patterns)

Along with the clothing, a rugged nylon belt is a must have. Leather belts absorb sweat and water. Remember, you may have to stand guard or patrol in the rain.

Footwear

Rugged, durable, as well as comfortable boots are another absolute. Boots will again be weather and terrain dependent. Water resistant boots are recommended for most of the United States terrain, minus the desert west and southwest. Insulated boots should be available for any terrain where snow and freezing temperatures are likely.

Team members who live in 4 Season climates should have both warm weather and cold weather boots. Boot laces must be checked and inspected regularly. Like the broken zipper or lost buttons, a broken boot lace during a security patrol will hamper the team members effectiveness. 550 cord is tremendous boot lace material and nearly indestructible. Regardless, every member should have spare boot laces.

* Rugged, thick socks are a must have for any weather. Wool and wool-blend socks are the best. Stay away from cotton and nylon socks, both will breed blisters on tired feet. Like sand in your eyes, a team member with blistered or raw feet will be out of commission and of no use to themselves or the team.

Foul Weather Gear

Emergencies and disasters do not cease because of wind, rain, and bad weather. All team members must be prepared to continue their mission regardless of bad weather.

Rain Poncho

The milspec rain poncho is versatile and useful. Forget about the discount, plastic ponchos at the local retail store, they will rip and be ruined after one use. Military surplus ponchos in various colors and camouflage patterns are readily available to your team anywhere in the USA.

Ponchos are preferable as they can be put on over uniforms, vests, and load-bearing gear. Team members will not have to strip down to put on a poncho and they are universally sized for all personnel. A poncho can also be quickly removed when the bad weather breaks. High winds are the enemy of the poncho.

Rain Suits

A rain suit allows for better movement and protects the lower half of the body more so than a poncho. A good rain suit, combined with water resistant boots can keep the wearer dry in the worst of weather, particularly high wind.

As mentioned, the downside of a rain suit is the fact that it is not designed to go over vests, holsters, and load-bearing gear. A suit takes longer to put on than a poncho, but it provides more protection from the elements.

Cold Weather Gear

As we mentioned in the boot section, if you live in a Four Season climate, you must be prepared to deal with the cold. Emergencies and disasters are not just warm weather events. Fleece is your friend and layers are the way to go. I have personally found that using an underlayer fleece jacket and the wind/waterproof rain suit has kept me warm in the snow and cold.

Regardless of the cold weather clothing you choose, it must be durable and loose enough to allow you to complete the mission, whatever that mission might be. Before you settle on a winter jacket, snow suit, etc. go to the range and see if you can employ your rifle and pistol effectively while wearing it. The downside to many cold weather jackets is that they tend to be tight in the arm/shoulder area.

Chapter 3　　Armament

Team Choices

"Your men must be well equipped."
Sun Tzu, Art of War

In the United States, there is a wide array of choices regarding calibers and styles of primary arms. The two primary calibers that should be considered by the Patriot Fire Team are 5.56mm (.223 Remington) or 7.62x39mm. Yes, the author is fully aware of all the others, however, for the sake of continuity, we must settle on a caliber and style that works for the team as a unit, and not concern ourselves with catering to individual preference.

Regarding arms in 5.56mm, the choice is simple; AR / M4 style and operating system. There are more magazines and accessories and spare parts for the Stoner-based AR firearm than any other style in the United States of America. This is matter of fact, not personal feeling or opinions.

The second most prevalent and popular arm is the Kalashnikov AK style. Again, magazines and ammunition are plentiful for this style of rifle or rifle caliber pistol (RCP). The AK is also very simple to operate and maintain.

Yes, the author is aware that to many American men, their choice of guns is often akin to a type of religion. Regardless of that fact, putting together a team where one man has an AR, another man has an AK, one guy uses his favorite SCAR Heavy, and the fourth guy carries a .30 Carbine is less than efficient to say the least.

A team is four men operating as a cohesive unit, not four guys acting as individuals. Regardless of personal preferences and feelings, a choice must be made. The PFT will either use 5.56mm AR style or 7.62x39mm AK style arms.

If such arms are out of the price range of the team members, then buy 4 Hi-Point 9mm carbines. I'm not kidding, It would be better for every man to use the same Hi-Point carbine than to have four individuals all carrying different long guns.

During the pages that follow, we will examine suggestions for both the AR team and the AK Team. I suppose, if your TL is a millionaire, he could buy everyone SCAR Heavy rifles, but that situation would be rare and unusual and that would still not address the spare parts and accessories issue.

Regardless of the particular weapon or rifle being carried, it is the responsibility of the team member to ensure that their firearms are cleaned, lubricated, and in excellent working order at all times. The safety and survival of the entire team and the success of the mission are reliant upon every man being thoroughly skilled with their primary weapon and the weapons of the other men on the team.

We refer back to the team concept. It is not enough for a man to be "good" with "his gun". In a team, every man is there to support the effort of every other man. There is no room on a team for a person who only cares about "his gun" or "his gear".

This is the law. The purpose of fighting is to win. There is no possible victory in defense. The sword is more important than the shield, and skill is more important than either. The final weapon is the brain. All else is supplementary.

- John Steinbeck

Team Leader (5.56mm AR)

The PFT Team Leader should be equipped with the necessary gear and equipment to effectively lead and maintain control over the team. At the same time, the Leader must be armed with the tools necessary to repel and defeat deadly threats to his team and by extension his community and his family.

The Leader will be carrying communications and signal gear as well other mission critical gear; compass/GPS, maps, etc. For this reason, the TL should gravitate toward a compact, and lighter primary arm, the RCP in 5.56 is a wise choice.

Primary Arm

A basic lightweight AR or Rifle Caliber Pistol with a stabilizing brace is preferable.

When using an RCP, barrel length of 10-11 inches is a good compromise between a full-sized rifle and a super-compact pistol. Super-short rifle barrels tend to be finicky when it comes to 5.56mm ammunition. Diminished accuracy and bullet-tumble are very real issues with the popular 7 inch barrels.

A sling is a must have accessory. Think of it as a holster for your rifle. The TL will often need one or both hands for other tasks. Setting the primary gun down to use comm or signal gear is a recipe for disaster.

Ammunition: the 77grain BTHP or Mk262 is the preferred 5.56mm load for dealing with human predators. In the author's experience, Black Hills Ammunition make the highest quality Mk262. This is what the US Army Special Forces uses. 55grain FMJ will work in a pinch. The 62grain "GreenTip" zips right through unarmored targets, but it is better than nothing.

Secondary Arm

A striker-fired, polymer framed, 9x19mm pistol, such as the GLOCK 19 is a near perfect size and weight. The holster must be rigid and rugged and accessible, even while wearing armor and load-bearing gear.

Ammunition: Any 115 grain or 124 grain duty-quality, controlled expansion ammo should work. Ball ammo is less effective and 147grain subsonic 9x19mm is best reserved for suppressed weapons.

Edge Weapons / Tools

The TL should have a sharp, rugged fixed blade knife on their person. However, it is not necessary to have a large or extra-large knife, like the Bowie or even a full-sized KaBar. Keep in mind that you need to carry all of your gear. Ounces add up to pounds and pounds can be pain.

Smoke/Flare Launcher

The TL is absolutely responsible for commands and signals for the team. Not all communication can be verbal or even audible. There are times when either smoke (day) or flares (night) are critical for signalling.

While smoke/flare launchers are not readily available in most gun stores, they can be found and purchased from specialty makers. Spikes Tactical makes several types of smoke and flare launchers in 37mm configuration.

37mm launchers and ammunition are "non-firearms" and do not fall under the category of firearms or explosives, therefore they can be ordered directly from the manufacturer. Unfortunately, many manufacturers of smoke and flare ammunition restrict sales (by choice, not law) to government agencies only.

Marine (boating, not USMC) supply stores are an excellent source of smoke and flare signaling devices. If nothing else, the TL should have an inexpensive Coast Guard approved flare pistol. These are normally orange and they fire easy to find 12 gauge signal flares. Handheld signalling smoke in various sizes can be found at boating stores as well.

If you are able to acquire a 37mm launcher, it will be up to you, the TL, to secure and test the variety of smoke, flare, are noise signalling ammunition that is available. It should also be noted that Spikes Tactical makes adapters to allow 12 gauge flares and 26.5 smoke/flare ammunition to be fired through their 37mm devices.

*Note - it is unlawful and a bad idea in general to attempt to fire standard 12 gauge ammunition from an aluminum flare launcher. If you need to fire 12 gauge buckshot, just buy a shotgun.

Team Leader with RCP and Launcher

Team Leader (7.62x39mm AK)

As previously discussed, the TL should have a compact, relatively lightweight primary arm. If PFT is using 7.62x39mm AK platform arms, the TL should select one of several Rifle Caliber Pistols with a stabilizing brace.

Primary Arm
Century Arms and a few others, offer both US made and imported RCP's with and without braces mounted. If your RCP does not have a brace, SB Tactical offers a few options for the AK-style.

Regarding accuracy with an AK-style RCP, the author has found that hits on man-sized silhouettes are practical out to 200 yards.

Aside from the primary arm being an AK chambered in 7.62x39mm, all other suggestions for the Team Leader armament discussed in the AR section still apply.

Ammunition: Most all 123 or 124 grain 7.62x39mm ammunition will suffice.

Secondary Arm

The Canik USA line of TP9 pistols come in full-sized, compact, and subcompact. They are less expensive than the GLOCK or SW M&P, but they are rhino-tough and extremely reliable.

Team Leader with AK - RCP

Automatic Rifleman (5.56mm AR)

As with the USMC model, the Automatic Rifleman is the team member who is relied upon to provide the greatest amount of firepower (fire volume) during a defensive situation. Consider the LA Riots of 1992 where dozens to hundreds of armed looters descended upon a neighborhood or business center. We saw this play out in Ferguson, Missouri in 2014 and Baltimore, Maryland where waves of thugs looted, burned, and destroyed anything in their path. Consider your family and neighborhood being in the path of a hoard of armed thugs and you and your team are the only thing between your families destruction and the mindless criminal monsters.

History Lesson: During the 1992 LA Riots, 63 people were killed and $800 million in damage was done to the city. Ferguson looting, arson, and robbery caused $4.6 million in damages. In Baltimore 113 police officers injured and $9 million in damages were committed by rioters. In all these incidents, innocent people were *irreparably harmed and innumerable families and businesses were bankrupted.*

Primary Arm

Requirements for the Automatic Rifleman's primar arm will be a long, heavy barrel capable of maintaining continuous fire for extended periods. Recommended barrel length is 20 inches with a muzzle device that helps control recoil and flash. For the sake of clarity, we will refer to the person of the Automatic Rifleman by the abbreviation AR and primary arm of that man as the Squad Automatic Weapon or SAW.

Feeding devices, magazines, for the SAW should be larger or of greater capacity than the standard team rifle. MagPul produced both 40 round magazines and 60 round drums for the AR. MagPul magazines are the current choice for the United States Marine Corps as a testament to their reliability and durability.

The SAW should be equipped with a strong sling. A padded sling is preferable as the gun will likely weigh ten to twelve pounds when it is loaded and ready to go. A bipod or similarly forward stabilizing device is also a must have for the SAW. The GripPod is a good choice. *Beware! There are cheap copies of the original MilSpec GripPod that are more likely than not prone to failure under hard use.

As large capacity magazines will not fit in standard rifle magazine pouches, the AR should carry a large sling pouch for spare ammunition.

The SAW must be in excellent working order and it is the responsibility of the Automatic Rifleman to ensure that his arm is clean and well-lubed constantly.

Ammunition: The SAW is the exception to the "Green Tip" rule. As the AR may have to engage vehicles as well as provide suppressive fire against hard targets, using 62 grain "Green Tip" in the team's SAW is a valid idea. This is also an area where red-tipped 5.56mm tracer ammunition has a practical application.

Secondary Arm

The AR may also carry a sidearm similar to the TL. Also, as with the TL, the AR should have a sharp, rugged knife on hand at all times.

Automatic Rifleman with heavy-barreled AR
and MagPul drum.

Automatic Rifleman (7.62x39mm AK)

For the team using the 7.62x39mm AK weapons, the Automatic Rifleman should be carrying a rifle similar to the RPK. An RPK is a Squad Automatic Weapon or SAW.

The RPK uses the same magazines as all standard 7.62 AK rifles and RCP's. The barrel is longer and heavier than a normal AK rifle. A quality RPK will have a solid, rugged stock, a bipod, and, often, a carrying handle. Again, a rugged, padded sling is a must have accessory.

Fortunately, large capacity magazines and drums for the RPK are readily available in 40 round, 75 round, and even 100 round configurations. *Note: AK drums are not top-loaded like standard rifle magazines and the AR must learn to load them properly.

Drum magazines are difficult to load in the field during a fight, therefore the standard operating procedure is to begin the engagement with a drum in place in the SAW and reload with either another drum or the 40 round magazines. It is tactical folly to save the large capacity magazines "for later".

An RPK, loaded with a 75 round drum will weigh ten to twelve pounds. As with 5.56mm SAW, the spare ammunition will need to be carried in a sling pouch or pack.

The Automatic Rifleman team member will be carrying the heaviest load of all. It should be readily apparent that the AR must possess the physical strength and stamina to carry all of this equipment. This is not the time to be timid or meek, if a man cannot carry the load, he cannot be the AR. As discussed at the outset of this section, the SAW is the most important firearm on the team.

Also, in the event that the Team Leader is injured or killed, the AR will assume the role of the TL and the SAW can be passed to the Assistant Automatic Rifleman.

Automatic Rifleman with RPK / Drum

Assistant Automatic Rifleman (5.56mm AR)

The Assistant Automatic Rifleman is, as the title indicates, responsible for aiding the Automatic Rifleman to keep the SAW up and running. The AAR will also carry a sling pouch or pack with extra ammunition for the SAW.

Primary Arm

The AAR will carry a standard configuration 5.56mm rifle with spare ammunition. The AAR, in addition to aiding the AR, may also be required to employ precision rifle fire as well as suppressive fire.

Additionally, the AAR must be completely familiar with the operation of the SAW in the event that the AR is injured or killed. We cannot call timeout in the middle of a gun battle. The SAW is so important to the mission of the Fire Team that there are two men designated to keeping it up and running.

Standard Tactical SOP will dictate that the AAR carries a spare drum for the SAW and additional magazines.

Secondary Arm

The AR may also carry a sidearm similar to the TL. Also, as with the TL, the AR should have a sharp, rugged knife on hand at all times.

Assistant Automatic Rifleman with CAR-15

Assistant Automatic Rifleman (7.62x39mm AK)

As with the 5.56mm AAR, the AK version is the immediate back up for the AR and must keep the SAW, in this case an RPK style, up and running.

Primary Arm

The AAR will carry a standard configuration AK. In the United States, both stamped receiver and milled receiver AK rifles are commonplace. The milled receiver guns will weigh a pound or more than stamped receiver guns. Also, an under folder or side folder version of the stamped AK may save the user a few ounces or more.

Regarding weight, before adding a heavy aluminum forend to your AK, consider the added weight penalty. Again, ounces equals pounds, pounds equal pain. No one is going to carry your gear for you. A standard underfolder AK will weigh around 7 pounds.

Secondary Arm

The AAR may also carry a sidearm similar to the TL. Also, as with the TL, the AR should have a sharp, rugged knife on hand at all times.

Assistant Automatic Rifle w Underfolder AK

Rifleman (5.56mm AR)

The Rifleman is the most utilitarian position and is the man most likely to be tasked with quick scouting or security missions. The Rifleman or simply, R, is also the back up to the Assistant Automatic Rifleman. In the event that any of the men up the chain are injured or killed, the R must step in and fill the AAR gap and support the AR to keep the SAW up and running. (Do we see a theme here?)

Primary Arm

The rifleman will carry a standard configuration AR style 5.56mm rifle. As with the AAR, the R may be called upon to provide precision rifle fire or covering suppressive fire. Standard load for the R will be his rifle, a *minimum* of 3 magazines in addition to the one in the rifle.

Unlike the TL or AR who have either short/compact rifles or long guns respectively, it is highly suggested that the rifle used by the designated team Rifleman be equipped with or capable of accepting a bayonet. When selecting a 5.56mm AR-style rifle, be aware that M4 Style carbines with 16 inch barrels, while technically equipped with a bayonet lug, have the lug recessed in such a way as to dramatically reduce the effectiveness of the bayonet. The M7 bayonet might not be cool or Gucci, but it is effective and rugged.

Before you view the bayonet as an anachronism from the Civil War, know this; you will encounter people who don't believe you would shoot them. However, the sight of a sharp, pointed piece of cold steel on the end of the rifle will make them think twice.

Secondary Arm

The Rifleman may also carry a sidearm similar to the TL. A sharp bayonet will work to fill the fixed blade knife requirement.

As the Rifleman will not be carrying the comm and signaling gear of the TL or the spare SAW ammo weight of the AR or AAR, the R may be tasked with carrying a larger, more comprehensive Medical Kit. All members will be carrying some form of personal trauma kit, but the R will carry a pouch or pack with additional med gear to be used by the entire team.

The Rifleman may also be dedicated as the team corpsman or medic. In the event of an injury, the R may provide medical assistance while the SAW is being kept up and running.

Rifleman with AR and bayonet

Rifleman (7.62x39mm AK)

The Rifleman on the AK configured team will have identical responsibilities to their 5.56mm counterpart.

Primary Arm

The Rifleman will be equipped with a standard 7.62x39mm AK rifle. Again, the consideration between stamped and milled receiver must be taken into account, though this is less critical than the AAR.   Standard load will be 3 magazines plus the one in the rifle for a total of 4 fully loaded magazines for the mission.

Regarding the attachment of a bayonet. You will have to be selective when purchasing an AK as many modern, particularly US made models do not have bayonet lugs. The good news is that Kalashnikov bayonets are not expensive and easy to find on the surplus market.

Secondary Arm

The Rifleman may also carry a sidearm similar to the TL. A sharp bayonet will work to fill the fixed blade knife requirement.

Once more, expect the AK Rifleman to carry additional medical supplies and other mission critical gear as designated by the Team Leader.

AK Rifleman with bayonet and snow poncho

Chapter 4   Specialties

Depending on the circumstances and mission at hand, there may be times when certain tactical specialties or specialists will be needed. During the next chapter will address specialists that may be called upon to aid in the successful completion of a mission.

"It is better to be a warrior in a garden than to be a gardener in a war."

Anonymous Warrior

Designated Marksman

Whether you call them sharpshooter, sniper, or designated marksman, the task of all is essentially the same; provide overwatch with precision rifle fire. A designated marksman or DM is a valuable asset for any team.

From a security standpoint, a DM can be posted as overwatch for roadblocks and checkpoints. The DM can provide overwatch for critical points on roads, bridges, gates, etc. In an urban environment, the DM is used as overwatch for security patrols, this is particularly important if hostile snipers are a real threat.

When I was a part of a contract security team with Blackwater, during the aftermath of Hurricane Katrina, it was common for the thug element to randomly fire from multi-story buildings and parking garages. The New Orleans thugs, in the beginning of the crisis, before strong men with black rifles arrived, went so far as to car jack the emergency utility trucks.

When hard men carrying black rifles arrived in mass, the blatant daytime thug activity diminished quickly and became a nocturnal activity for the most part. Lesson: when looters and rioters realized that there were men who would shoot back, it was not so much fun anymore.

Naturally, any person who would be a DM will need to have a better than average amount of skill with a rifle. It does not matter how much money you spent on a rifle, it is the operator that counts. The other men in the team must be absolutely confident that the man on overwatch is the best shooter, as their lives may very well depend on the skills of the man behind the rifle.

Primary Arm: Urban Environment

The urban DM should be able to effectively employ an accurized AR-15 style rifle. By accurized, we mean a free-floated barrel with a match crown, a precision trigger tuned to 3.5 to 4 pounds, a minimum 10x riflescope with external adjustments, an adjustable stock (preferable, but not absolute) and an adjustable bipod.

Ammunition

Depending on the rifling of the barrel, the 77grain Mk262 is a prime choice for the DM rifle. However, some precision rifles will shoot the lighter bullets better. The USMC has an OTM Mk318 5.56mm load that uses a 62grain bullet. Federal Ammunition loads this and it is available for civilian purchase.

Primary Arm: Suburban / Open Country Environment

For the open country environment, the DM may be better served with a rifle chambered in .308 Winchester. Precision bolt-action rifles, such as an accurized Remington 700 fit the bill nicely. The same precision rifle requirements apply to the .308 as the 5.56mm rifle.

Ammunition

Fortunately, 168 and 175 grain match grade BTHP ammunition for the .308 Winchester rifle is readily available from most any company that sells ammunition. Again, Black Hills Ammunition is the premium. Federal Cartridge is also a solid choice for match grade rifle ammo.

Designated Marksman blending in.

Corpsman/Medic

Every team member should be skilled in basic field trauma medicine and be able to address the big three killers; major hemorrhage, loss of airway, and tension pneumo-thorax (TPX). A medic or corpsman will have a greater knowledge and ability to deal with most any injury or illness that a team might experience.

The best selection for a team medic would be a person with formal education and real world experience. If you are so lucky to have a US Navy Combat Corpsman or a Special Forces Medic (18D) you are way ahead of the game. Civilian EMTs and Paramedics are also good choices. Nurses and doctors are great, but their shortcoming is that they work in fully equipped buildings with lots of machines and support staff. The PFT medic will be working in the field out of a backpack.

The PFT medic is someone who can deal with more than what the normal TCCC (Tactical Combat Casualty Care) training gets into. Your medic will run IVs, pass meds when need be, stitch or staple wounds, address broken bones, etc.

Every PFT member should have in their possession at a minimum; tourniquet(s), pressure dressings, NPA (nasopharyngeal airway), stainless steel decompression needle, duct tape, gauze, and chest seal material.

A Medic's bag will have oral airways, sutures and needles, IV fluid and tubing, splints/braces, shears, scalpels, eye wash, burn gel, extra PPE (personal protective equipment), space blankets, and much more. Another big plus in our modern world is the availability of canned oxygen. These disposable O2 cans come in small, medium, and large sizes and can be a big help when the physical stress is high.

One of the most important roles for the PFT Medic/Corpsman is to care for, not just team members, but their families and neighbors. A good medic can deal with non-life threatening injuries and ailments to keep the whole community healthy. Small cuts, scrapes, and splinters can seem minor, but they can also become infected quickly and lead to much bigger problems. I know corpsmen and medics who have also assisted in childbirthing when it was just too late to get to a hospital. Remember, during the crisis or emergency, you will not always be able to rely on standard care.

Even your neighbors who have been leery or on the fence about your "patriot militia" will be quickly won over when your medic bandages up their injured kid or gives care to their wife.

Corpsman Kit w/ Oxygen

Bonus Material

Citizen 9-Line Medic Request

1. Where are you? (Address, Landmark, Mile Marker etc.)

2. Patient still breathing

3. Number injured

4. Describe the accident / Method of Injury

5. Special considerations for first responders (Trapped person, Fire etc.)

6. Hazards in the area? (Chemical Spill, Crime in progress etc)

7. Method of marking area (Hazard lights, flashlight, flare)

8. Your name

9. Your phone number

Breacher

There may be times, particularly during an ongoing emergency/crisis (riots and civil unrest, etc) that your team may have to get into a building or area in a hurry in order to ensure the safety and security of innocent people. During the aftermath of an earthquake, tornado, or hurricane, innocent victims may be trapped inside of damaged structures. How are you going to get in and tend to the critically injured and trapped people?

For manual, non-explosive, breaching there are a number of tools that are readily available to the PFT team that can be extremely useful. In addition to normal clothing and gear that we have previously discussed, let's take a moment to consider some of the more specialized gear that will be a bit more mission specific.

Breacher Gear

Sledgehammer: a breachers hammer should be in the 3 to 5 pound range with a short handle. (A 12 pound, long-handled sledge might seem great until you have to carry it any distance) Polymer handles are preferable to wood, but wood will work if that is all you have.

Pry Bar: There are a tremendous number of pry bars available. Military, Fire, and Police call these "Halligan" or "Hooligan" tools. Combined with medium-weight sledge, the Halligan can be the "master key" for breaching. Of course, that method requires two men, not one.

Bolt Cutters: A solid set of bolt cutters can help the breacher to rapidly remove standard padlocks, cut through fencing, and other obstructions.

12 Gauge Shotgun: ballistic breaching can be accomplished with a 12 gauge, pump action shotgun if the operator is skilled in its use. Frangible (compressed copper powder) slugs will disperse instantly upon impact, thus reducing the hazard of splashback. However, they are not cheap and you will not find them at

the local hardware store. Birdshot can be used, with caution. Foster slugs might seem like the ultimate in power, but the hazard of ricochet and lead splash is HIGH. (Yes, I've been there and been fragged)

The breacher shotgun should be compact for easy maneuvering in tight quarters. Pistol grips or "bird head" grips are preferable. The Mossberg "Shockwave" guns are good choices. The breacher will want a sling on the gun as he will likely need to free up his hands in a hurry for other tasks .

CAUTION: Pressing the muzzle directly against an object can cause the barrel to violently rupture. Some type of "stand off" device at the muzzle reduces this risk. Again, Mossberg has commercially available guns with stand-offs. *Personal protective gear; eye wear, ear muffs, and gloves are absolutes for a breacher.

The Breacher will want some type of pack/rig for their specialty gear. A pouch or loops for shotgun shells will also be valuable.

As the breacher will be toting a fair amount of weight, they will forgo a long gun. The 12 gauge shotgun can be used as a fighting tool and a pistol can be carried in a rigid holster.

Torches, power saws (circular and chain) are naturally heavy and cumbersome, but may be kept on hand by the team. Chainsaws are a must have for clearing debris in the aftermath of severe storms and natural disasters.

Going back to the leery or suspicious neighbors, if your team uses a chainsaw(s) to clear debris from the neighborhood, that puts you right back into the hero category.

Breacher w/ compact 12 gauge shotgun

Crowd Control

Not every problem or threat can, or should be, solved ballistically. During the crisis or emergency, you may encounter hostile people who must be dispersed with less-than-lethal means.

Thanks to the prevalence of bears in the United States, large canisters of "bear spray" are widely available at most all outdoor/sporting goods stores, particularly in the west. Bear Spray is composed of Oleoresin Capsicum, better known as pepper spray. OC/Pepper Spray is a fantastic, less-than-lethal force alternative.

The primary concern with less-than-lethal use of force is for the operator to understand when to employ it, versus lethal force. Less-than-lethal force should not be attempted as a means to seem "reasonable" or "nice". If the threat or threats are carrying weapons, whether firearms, edged weapons, or bludgeons, that is a deadly force situation. One man, with bear spray, against a crowd wielding knives and baseball bats will be quickly overwhelmed and severely injured or killed.

The 37mm launcher, if chosen by the Team Leader, can also be loaded with smoke, noise-makers, and CS or OC canisters, if you are fortunate enough to get your hands on them. When used in conjunction, smoke and CS put thugs and looters on notice as they will never know which is which and will learn to avoid them.

However, it must be understood that looters/rioters who decide to push ahead, despite the use of less-than-lethal means, are determined to cause harm to innocents. Refer back to your Use of Force training. When the good guy is outnumbered by bad men, that becomes a Deadly Force scenario. If twenty rioters attempt to overwhelm a four man PFT, they are demonstrating Deadly Force intent and must be dealt with accordingly. Keep in mind, a PFT is under no obligation to attempt arrest or to minimize use of force in order to protect those threatening them.

*Refer to the original Patriot Fire Team manual for detailed explanation of Justifiable Use of Force and the definition of Deadly Force.

Chapter 5 Food and Water

Regardless of the crisis or emergency, you are still a human animal and you need to eat and drink. Food is discussed in great detail in the original PFT Manual. MRE's are good food for the field, as you can eat them on the go. Depending on your mission, you may or might not pack out food when you step off.

Nutrition equals energy and energy is what you will need to function and survive during a crisis. When I was a grunt, I learned to stash MRE food packages on my person so that I could eat whenever I had a chance.

Regarding water and how to carry it, there are many options available. The standard plastic canteen still works as well today as it did forty years ago. Water bladders that ride in a backpack kind of configuration are convenient and work well also. Of course, the fall back is to simply pack out store-bought bottles of water in some kind of pouch or pack.

SWAT Fuel .40 Cal Multivitamins and their 9mm +P endurance formula can and will give you the boost you need during crisis situations. Remember, during an emergency, your mind and body will be taxed to a far greater extent than you are used to.

The amount of water your team members will carry will depend on a number of factors; climate, temperature, anticipated length of the mission, resupply options, condition of the men, etc.

If you are operating in a rural, field environment and anticipate resupplying your water from creeks or streams, some type of water purification accessories are absolutes. You will not likely have the time to boil water to kill the bacteria. Even if the water is moving and looks "clean" there is a good chance that it contains some kind of bacteria that will upset your insides. A man with diarrhea or the GI term: "dysentery", will be out of action and of no use to the team. Severe dysentery combined with exposure and lack of nutrition will kill men in the field.

Look at the number of soldiers who died in the Civil War from dysentery versus bullets. In fact, diarrhea and dysentery alone claimed more men than did battle wounds. This fact is not unique to the Civil War. Disease often kills more men during wars and conflicts than rifles, artillery, and bombs.

Chapter 6

Field Sanitation and Hygiene

Keeping with the dangers of illness and disease, the Team Leader and Corpsman must be diligent and unrelenting with regard to enforcing field sanitation and personal hygiene. This is critical for the unit's strength and survival during difficult emergency situations.

Physical and emotional stress take a toll on the human body. When the body is under stress, tired, malnourished, it lacks the ability to fight off the germs and bacteria that it would easily have been able to defeat under normal circumstances. Have you ever had a few bad nights where you failed to get a good amount of sleep and then ended up getting a cold? Exposure to the elements doesn't make you sick, but the stress that the exposure puts on your body reduces its ability to fight off the sickness.

The Team Leader and his assistants must designate latrine/bathroom areas if the normal toilet facilities are not available. You cannot have men peeing and crapping all over the place. Food waste, human waste, and garbage must be disposed of and preferably burned to keep away the rats, mice, flies, etc. that can spread disease like wildfire.

Handwashing and toothbrushing are not just niceties, they are critical for keeping the body healthy. Don't let you men eat with unwashed hands. Brushing your teeth removes bacteria from the mouth and helps to maintain overall good health.

Socks and undergarment should be changed regularly to prevent chafing and a build up of moisture on the feet and in the crotch. I got a case of "crotch rot" during infantry school. It was summer in coastal North Carolina and no one told me not to wear cotton underwear to the field. Later, I learned to "freeball" in the field when it was hot and humid.

This is not a joking matter. Your security team could literally be the difference between life and death for your family and community during the aftermath of a catastrophe or crisis. If your team cannot function because all or several members are sick, who will guard those who cannot protect themselves?

Chapter 7 Access Denial

During the immediate aftermath of a natural disaster or an ongoing man made disaster (RIOT) there will likely be a need to limit, restrict, or deny access to your community / neighborhood. An extremely typical tactic of urban thugs is to branch out and attack neighborhoods and communities while existing law enforcement is occupied with concentrated rioting and looting in one area, generally the downtown.

For example, during the LA Riots of 1992, violence began as a localized event, but it rapidly spread to adjacent communities including Inglewood, Hawthorne, Compton, and Long Beach. After the initial assault on the downtown area, looters will typically load up en mass in vehicles and head to the suburbs to take advantage of the chaos and victimize those who might normally be out of line of fire. They do this knowing full well that the 911 system has been overloaded and police response will be either extremely delayed or non-existent.

In order to restrict access to only those with a legitimate need to be in your neighborhood, you will need physical barriers that can be rapidly put into place. The PFT will need to set up checkpoints and roadblocks to address the very real threat of looters overwhelming the community. Remember, your wives and children will be in your homes. The best way to keep them safe is to keep the fight away from your houses. Waiting for gangbangers to kick in your front door is not an effective security strategy.

During the pages that follow we will offer solutions for Access Denial barriers and checkpoint material. These suggestions are based upon material that should be readily available at your local home improvement and farmer supply stores.

*For Informational and Educational Purposes

Checkpoints

Vehicles as Barriers

The fastest way to block off a street (the entrance to a neighborhood) is to pull a vehicle or vehicles across the roadway. The advantage to this method is that it can be done quickly with essentially no physical labor. The downside is that these vehicles become "sacrificial lambs" as they will be subject to being rammed by looter vehicles or shot up by armed thugs.

If you are relying on your pickup truck to transport supplies for your family, you don't want to sacrifice it to a riot demolition derby or allow it to become a bullet sponge for thugs armed with all the guns they stole from a pawn shop. If you have old, junk vehicles that can be put in place, use them. Don't sacrifice useful, utility vehicles.

Road Spikes

Spike Board: An easy to make and easy to deploy road spike barrier can be made by taking a standard 1x6 piece of lumber and driving 60 penny (6 inch) or 70 p (7 inch) carpentry nails through the board and staggering them. The average 1x6 board is 8 feet long.

Drill a hole on each end of the board and loop a rope through each hole so that it can be put in place or pulled out of the way by friendly forces quickly. Depending on the width of the road, you may choose to use one, two, or three of these Spike Boards. (Skill Level: Beginner)

Caltrops / Jack Rocks: Using the previously discussed 60p or 70p nails, you can produce individual road spikes that can be deployed en mass on roadways just beyond barriers or signs forbidding people to enter the road. When spread widely over a likely avenue of approach, caltrops have the added advantage of greatly slowing the advance of mobs of looters. The loots will not be able to run at or rush defenders, that is unless they want to impale their feet on the spikes. These will not stop them, but will definitely slow their roll.

To make individual road spikes, take 2 large nails and cut off the head to create an angled point. Bend the nails approximately 45 degrees and weld the two nails together at the bends so that no matter how they land, one point will be up. Think of a child's toy jacks, only much larger. (Skill Level: Intermediate to Advanced)

There are a few online outlets that sell premade caltrops. One store sells them in ten packs for $50. You will likely need dozens or even hundreds, at $5 piece that price tag adds up quickly. It might be a good idea to purchase some and then replicate more later.

PS: "Jack Rocks" is the term that union men use for road spikes that they litter around the gates during labor disputes. The Japanese call these devices tetsubishi and they date back to the feudal era. One form of caltrop, that looked more like a large toy jack, was widely used during the American Civil War to impede cavalry troops.

Signs and Barriers

Sawhorses: The typical sawhorse made of 2x4 lumber can be quickly assembled and used to mount traffic control signs at checkpoints. During a crisis, if you don't have a Stop sign for your roadblock you can surely find one at an intersection somewhere. A sturdy sawhorse can be drug in and out of the road quickly.

A large sign affixed to a sawhorse that states "Looters Will Be Shot" might seem a bit dramatic, however, the middle of a riot is not the time to be sensitive. "Looters Will Be Shot" is a warning that cannot be misconstrued even by the most sub-moronic thug.

Hedgehog: A hedgehog looks like a giant caltrop or tetsubishi. During WWI and WWII hedgehogs were constructed of steel "I" beam material to impede tanks on roads and landing craft on beaches. For our purposes, we can make hedgehogs out of 4x4 lumber. You will need 3 - 4 foot pieces of 4x4, heavy duty bolts and/or 90° corner braces/brackets (heavy duty) and wood screws that are at least 3 inches long.

Lay two pieces of 4x4 centered atop one another in a "+" sign configuration. Secure them together with a heavy duty bolt. Now take the third piece of 4x4 and center it on the other two, making a three-dimensional cross or "t". When it is complete you have your six-pointed wooden hedgehog. If you require larger hedgehogs just alter the length of your 4x4. (Skill Level: Beginner)

After you have made several wooden hedgehogs you can spread them out and run barbed wire between them to create a barrier that can be quickly deployed across a road. While it is true that a hedgehog will not stop a car or truck, any person that drives over one, particularly when wrapped in barbed wire, is not going to be happy.

Hedgehogs from common lumber

55 Gallon Drums: If you need to create barriers that with stop or slow down vehicles, 55 gallon drums are an easy solution. A 55 gallon drum filled with water will weigh around 450 pounds. If you set them up in a triangle formation that gives you 1300 plus pounds of barrier.

Conversely, if you can get your hands on steel 55 gallon drums and fill them with sand, each one will weigh over 800 pounds. Put the sand filled drums in a triangle formation and you have over *one full ton* of weight. That will slow down any standard passenger car or light truck. Steel drums filled with sand will naturally provide cover from small arms fire as well.

Sandbags: Sandbags are easy to come by and not that expensive. You can purchase the industrial variety that will be white, orange or some other color. The surplus market also is a good place to find military OD green sandbags. Naturally, plain white sandbags are the least expensive. Expect to pay $30 to $40 for 100 white sandbags.

Sandbags have been used to build cover for armies for a hundred years or more. They are versatile but they are also labor intensive to fill. Filling sandbags is definitely a team project. Note: In the event of an ongoing crisis, you must remember to maintain security during the construction process. Double thick walls of sandbags should stop any conventional small arms you might be facing (.50 BMG is a different story).

When reinforcing guard posts or checkpoints with sandbags, the normal configuration will be a "U" or three-sided square with the opening facing the secure area. The sandbag wall should be built up to the sternum of the average man; think 4 to 4.5 feet tall. (Skill Level: Beginner)

If at any time you might think this preparation is excessive or paranoid, consider the option of having your neighborhood overrun by fifty to a hundred armed thugs. Think about watching your family run crying from your burning house. Imagine your wife and daughter being repeatedly raped while your dead body grows cold twenty feet away. Now, get back to work preparing your team.

Razor Wire and Barbed Wire: Barbed wire is available at any home or farm supply store. For instance, when this was written, an 80 Rod (440 yards) spool of barbed wire was $50 at Tractor Supply. The down side to barbed wire is that it is not self supporting. You will need engineer stakes, wooden posts, or something like the hedgehog we discussed previously. The upside is the cost effectiveness and versatility.

Razor wire comes in rolls and is self-supporting. You can stretch out a roll of razor wire and it stands up. The diameter of the rolls of razor wire will vary from 12 inches all the way up to 36 inches. On the commercial market, 18 inch rolls of razor wire seem to be the most common. Like the barbed wire, you can order and pick up razor wire at home and farm stores. You can even get it from Walmart or Amazon. Remember to purchase a few pairs of thick "Wire Handling Gloves". Your hands will thank you. (Skill Level: Intermediate)

Barbed and razor wire are primarily used to deny/restrict access to people on foot. Yes, a car or truck could drive over/through wire, but the tires won't last very long. Imagine the rushing mob scenario. How do you slow down fifty armed looters with only a few men? Even in a deadly force situation, you will find it difficult at best to address forty or fifty threats, all at once.

Regardless of how motivated, cracked up, or angry a mob might be, they are not going to be happy campers when they run into triple thick rows of razor wire. Even if they attempt to breach the razor wire with ladders, discarded house doors, or lumber, that will take time and it also creates a funnel point on which the defenders can focus. Razor wire can be cut with heavy duty tools, something thugs are not likely to have. Cutting through barbed or razor wire is again a time consuming affair, giving the defenders time to react to the threat.

Trip Flares and Noisemakers

Tripwire alarms have been around a long, long time. The Vietnam War is largely responsible for popularising trip flares or tripwire audible alarms. These devices are simple concepts. You have a spring-loaded striker held in place by a pin attached to a length of thin wire or even fishing line. When "tripped" the pin comes out, the striker hits a primer and either a flare launches or a super-loud, blank cartridge goes "Boom!"

Imagine a perfectly still, quiet night. It's 0230 and your night watch sentry is struggling to stay awake. Out of nowhere, Boom! The sound of a 12 gauge shotgun blank shatters the night. Or, there is a heavily used walking trail that leads to your property. Two hundred yards from your fence line you mount trip flares across the trail. Again, the middle of night; bang, woosh, a bright red flare streaks through the blackened sky. Bingo, someone or some ones is/are busted.

At present, 12 gauge marine flares and 12 gauge blank cartridges are the easiest to find for the non-military person. There are several companies that offer ready made "bear alarms" or "sonic alarms" and they are priced modestly.

Tripwire flares or noise alarms are best utilized by placing them across likely avenues of approach. They also act as a force multiplier because you will not be able to everywhere at all times. Trip wires can also be attached to rarely used gates, side entrances, etc. Also, they can be attached to things you might need to store outside, but a thief would want to steal; portable propane tanks come immediately to mind.

Naturally, all of the team members need to be aware of the placement of tripwire alarms. They won't injure them, but they might cause involuntary bladder evacuation and then your surprise is ruined. If a friendly or an enemy activates a tripwire alarm you will need to relocate it. Also, from an OpSec (Operational Security) standpoint, you will want to install your tripwire alarms when prying eyes cannot

observe you. This may mean installing them
after the sun has set.

Chapter 8

Strength and Fitness

By the time you have reached this point in the book it should be obvious that you will need some strength and physical fitness if you hope to carry your personal gear load and operate as a part of a team. A lesson that I learned early on during my time in the Marine Corps, and one that was continuously reinforced, was that no one else cared if I was tired or hungry. The hungry part was discussed earlier. The strength part is what we will focus on right now.

The armor, guns, and other gear that are necessary for the defense of your family and community are going to be heavy. They will be even heavier if your fitness level is poor. No one is going to carry your gear for you.

We don't expect you to hump or ruck twenty-five miles with a full combat load the first day out. Nonetheless, you will need to be able to physically support your personal load, even if you are just standing guard at the intersection to your neighborhood. When you get tired and fatigued your mental focus diminishes and you are more prone to making costly mistakes.

Step One: Put on your personal body armor and go for a walk. If you are worried about people seeing you with a plate carrier, wear an oversized button up shirt or sweatshirt over it. You may discover early on that you need to adjust the armor carrier. It should fit snugly against your body, but not be so tight that your arms fall asleep. The carrier should ride high up on your chest, not down around your belly.

The muscles used to support a plate carrier or even a backpack are different than the ones you use on a daily basis. They are also different from the ones you use at the gym when you bench and curl.

While strong arms are nice to have, a strong back and strong legs will pay huge dividends when it comes to carrying a heavy load. If you are the guy that views "leg day" as a rare occasion, you need to rethink your training.

Step Two: You need to alter your fitness thought process and understand that true strength comes from understanding that everyday is leg day. Barbell squats are the most important exercise you can do to strengthen your legs and back. If you have only squatted and/or deadlifted on rare occasions now is the time to change the way you think. Starting Strength, Edition 3 by Mark Rippetoe is a must read book. This will give you the psychological reinforcement you need to get on the correct path.

Step Three: Get some coaching. If you are like most men, and I used to be in that category, you assume that you know what you are doing and can just mimic what you have seen in the gym. That is akin to trying to learn how to shoot from watching other people. My good friend, Matt Reynolds, runs a program called Barbell Logic Online Coaching. Follow the link (if you are reading the digital version) or go to their site and read the basic info. Matt has a cadre of arguably the best strength coaches in the United States. (If you decide to sign up, use the "SOTG" promo code and save money)

Barbell Logic coaches will guide you through the beginner stages and help you to be the strongest human that you can possibly be, regardless of age or current physical condition. You will rapidly discover that you might not know as much as you thought and that is a good thing.

Aerobic or cardiovascular fitness can be gained relatively quickly. The downside is that it is lost just as fast. Gaining genuine strength takes time, but it stays with you much longer if you have to take time off.

The kind of strength and fitness we are focusing on here has nothing to do with ego or looking cool at the gym. You cannot wait until the emergency or crisis to decide you are going to get strong. Just like gear, if you don't have it when the crisis hits, it is too late to get it.

Trust me, it does not matter how old you are or what kind of physical ailments you have, you can get stronger. When I was a police officer, I injured my left shoulder fighting with and arresting some assholes. That injury became chronic and every time I thought it was healed, the pain would come back. I thought that my days of benching or even doing push ups were over. I also had chronic lower back pain. Matt taught me how to lift correctly. I am now squatting, deadlifting, and bench pressing, things I never thought I would be able to do again.

Now is the time to start getting strong.

Chapter 9 Night Ops

Depending on the season and your locale, at least half of the time it is going to be dark. Believe it or not, bad guys don't take a break and cease their evil ways because the sun went down. You must be able to deal with intrusions and assaults during hours or darkness.

Referring back to my time in New Orleans, post Katrina, for the first week or so it was a free-for-all, looting and outright robbery went on all hours of the day and night. However, when hard men with rifles arrived, the vermin almost immediately moved to nocturnal activities.

During the aftermath of a major environmental disaster; hurricane, tornado, earthquake, etc. the power grid will most certainly be interrupted. This interruption could be days or weeks. On the Gulf Coast, many areas were without reliable power for weeks after Katrina. Hurricane Katrina also destroyed many utility poles and power lines so even when the power was back on, many areas were still dark for months afterward at night. I recall driving along the coast around Biloxi, Mississippi more than a year after the hurricane and it was black as midnight for miles.

Flashlights

Every person on the team should have both a high quality, tactical type flashlight capable of projecting a beam for fifty yards or more. Think 500 lumen as a good place to start. Many 1000 lumen LED lights are available at reasonable prices.

The downside to high powered lights is that they are battery suckers. You will need a lower powered utility light to perform more mundane tasks. An LED headlamp, that only puts out perhaps 50 lumen, will last for hours and hours of continued use. Such lights are available at most camping/outdoor stores and they run on easy to find AA or AAA batteries.

Speaking of batteries, buy more batteries than you think you might need AND buy American, not cheap Chinese batteries. Chinese batteries have ruined many otherwise good lights.

Quality American-made 123A Lithium batteries have a 10 year shelf life as well.

Battery powered LED lanterns are a good choice for home use. They are safer than candles and oil lamps. You have enough problems to worry about without fearing your kids will burn the house down with candles.

Glow-sticks or Chemlights fall into the same category as batteries regarding quality. Chinese glow-sticks are fun for the kids at Halloween, but they won't last long on the shelf. American made mil-spec Chemlights are more pricey, but they will actually work when they are needed.

Night Vision

Thanks in large part to the Global War on Terror (a lot of money spent on development) and the natural advancements in technology, night vision equipment is available to the average citizen, not just the Special Operations Unit spending government money. Not very long ago, genuine night vision gear, the good stuff, was priced beyond what most people could afford. Today, that has changed.

Before we dive too far into the subject of night vision gear, we need to understand that there are two basic types of night vision; Starlight or NODs (Night Optical Devices) and Thermal Imagers.

Starlight / NODs

A "starlight scope" is an electronic optical device that magnifies available light thousands of times beyond what the human eye is capable. When I was first in the Marine Corps, the ANPVS-4's and PVS-5's were the top of the line in starlight. Today, the PVS-14 is the standard.

A starlight scope is passive, that is, it gathers the available light and magnifies it for the operator, allowing them to see what could not be seen with their naked eye. Infrared light is an active type of light that is not visible to the human eye but it is picked up by the NOD. The downside of using IR light to aid your starlight optic is that anyone else using a similar device can see it. As mentioned, standard night vision is passive, it does not throw out a beam.

Traditional NODs allow the user to view the world in shades of green. It is as if you are watching a black and white TV, but instead of shades of gray, you see shades of green. Most starlight rifle scopes today use a red colored reticle to stand out from the green. Recently, digital night vision has become available that offers multiple colors, not just green. Digital night vision has reduced the end user cost, but it is not quite up to the level of the military Generation III+ NODs as far as clarity is concerned.

Night vision products can be as simple as a monocular or binocular used to scan an area to the more complex and specialized for mounting on rifles. A simple monocular can be had for less than $1000, many are available for less than $500. However, this is definitely a time when you get what you pay for. When it comes to night vision, the more you spend, the greater the clarity and better the depth perception. Depth perception problems were the big issue with older NODs. Many helicopters crashed because pilots flying with NODs could not properly gauge distance.

Thermal Imagers

Thermal imagers are, as the name indicates, devices that sense variations in temperature. Living creatures, animals and humans, produce a heat signature that stands out from plants, water, and nonliving surroundings like dirt, concrete, etc. Unlike a night vision device that simply amplifies non-visible light, a thermal imager picks up heat. Thermal imagers work regardless of the light conditions because they are not dependent on visible or invisible light.

Thermals pick up humans better at night because the surroundings are naturally cooler when the sun goes down. If you have good light from artificial or natural sources, you really don't need thermal. Thermal imagers are most beneficial when the sun is down or indoors when the lights are out. You might say that a thermal imager can help you sneak around in buildings without the need for flashlights or IR.

Just as with starlight, the more you spend the better imagery you will get. I have used thermal imagers in the $10,000 range that allowed the user to clearly "see" a human threat in complete darkness hiding in the basement of a building.

As with the starlight or NODs, you can buy thermal imagers that are handheld, just for scanning an area, you can purchase helmet mounted units that are mounted in front of your face or you can use a thermal scope and affix it to a rifle.

Thermal imaging technology is more expensive than starlight. Expect to pay just under a thousand dollar for a monocular or handheld scanner and several thousand dollars for a thermal riflescope.

The down side of shopping for night vision of any kind is that there are so many different brands and types available that the purchaser can be confused and frustrated over what to buy. In general, if the price seems too good to be true, it probably is. A Generation I (one) night optic device will let you see what you could not with your naked eye, but the image will be relatively blurry and the effective distance will likely be limited to less than 100 yards. Conversely, a Generation III+ device will allow almost crystal clear viewing and allow you to monitor several hundred to a thousand yards out.

Is some type of night vision device, whether traditional or thermal, worth the investment? That is entirely up to you. However, if you already have your rifle, pistol, armor, etc. I would strongly consider, before you buy another gun, the value of being able to see in the dark. What lessons have we learned from the past? When armed men are present during the daytime, bad men will become nocturnal.

Chapter 10 The Community

Something that must be kept in mind at all times is that the Patriot Fire Team must function as a part of the community. While that statement might seem obvious on the face, nonetheless, it must be said.

Regardless of all the guns, gear, supplies, etc. that you might possess, your greatest strength in a disaster or a crisis is a strong community. Though the PFT members have volunteered to be the watchdogs for the neighborhood, they still need to commune with neighbors and community members.

One of the many lessons I learned from being a policeman was to be nice to the clerks at the 24 hour Quicky Mart. My first Police Chief would always go out of his way to stop in at the local quick shop and chit chat with the clerks. It used to annoy me when I was with him because I was young and full of testosterone. I wanted to be out chasing bad guys.

One day my Chief said, "The local business people are our eyes and ears. They see as much or more of what is going on in the neighborhood than we do. If they offer you a cup of coffee, say 'thank you' and take it." As I began to pay closer attention, I would realise how we would get tips and information from the local business people that we could not have gotten on our own. We got tips about car break-ins, vandalism, dope dealing, etc.

Some cops, particularly state troopers, would get their ass hairs up when a local quick shop or restaurant tried to give them a "free" coffee. They would insist on paying full price out of moral righteousness. My Chief explained that the free cup of coffee, that might cost the business 25 cents, was their way of saying "thank you". When the aforementioned troopers refused, they were really refusing the thanks of the local business. Essentially, they said, "Stick your thanks up your ass." Those locals business people would immediately view said cop as a "jerk" or "dick". No community intel or cooperation would be forthcoming.

Keep in mind, I'm talking about a cup of coffee or a fountain soda, not free meals or envelopes stuffed with cash. The simple fact is, you need the community to be on your side if you want to be an effective protector. Alienating them just makes your job more difficult.

By the time you have reached this far in the text, I am assured that you now understand the importance of having a team of trained, equipped, and prepared men to protect your community. As a leader, you cannot assume that everyone in your community will come to that realization, at least not immediately.

People on the outside will be concerned and want to know what your "militia" is all about. The simplest answer for the uneducated is to tell them that your group is like a Neighborhood Watch program for community emergencies. Truthfully, the PFT is like a Neighborhood Watch with rifles, armor, and dedicated training.

When do you go public about your PFT group; before or after the crisis hits? That question needs serious consideration.

If you live in a community that is filled with liberal, big government solutions, anti-gun activists, announcing publicly that you are training a group of armed, neighborhood security members will put you in the crosshairs. Yes, we all know that those same people will come begging for protection when the looters, rioters, and armed gangs are at the gate. If the previous circumstance is the case, your best option is to keep your PFT training and organization activities close to the vest.

Conversely, if you live in free America, a state that has Constitutional Carry and you know the majority of your neighbors are gun-carriers and patriots, your task is much simpler.

Regardless of your current community circumstance, you can begin with a simple gesture. If you are a member of a church community, organize a potluck/carry-in dinner or have a spaghetti supper, whatever. If not a church, use your local community center, VFW hall, etc. Food always brings people together.

Set up the meal, and when everyone is full, offer a no-charge educational discussion or talk. I mentioned this in detail in the Legion of Michael church security manual. The topic should be simple and easy for people to understand. Keep the discussion to about forty-five minutes or so. Any longer and you risk losing their attention.

Potential topics could be; life-saving trauma training "This is a tourniquet and this is how it works." If you have a pro-liberty Sheriff, ask them or their Chief Deputy to give a talk about home security tips. You might do a less-than-lethal self-defense seminar extolling the benefits of certain tools; pepper spray etc. You might also have someone give a gardening or food canning discussion.

Keep in mind that it is not necessary at all to bring up or discuss the Patriot Fire Team model. The community dinner is not about recruiting for the PFT, you already did that. The dinner/get-together is like the Police Chief stopping to chit chat with the quick stop clerks or the small business owners. You are building a community of people who will be predisposed to work with you when the crisis arrives, and it will, sooner or later.

PFT Symbology

The symbols used for the Patriot Fire Team come from the Marine Corps. These symbols are used on range cards and diagrams to indicate individual team members.

The Circle with a Slash is the Team Leader.

The Circle with the Arrow is the Automatic Rifleman.

The Circle with the "A" is the Assistant Automatic Rifleman.

The empty Circle is the Rifleman.

Additional Books for Patriots

From Paul G. Markel

Patriot Fire Team Manual

Examining the Armed Citizen

Faith and the Patriot

Legion of Michael: Defending the Flock

Also, go to:

WWW.PATRIOTBOOKSHELF.COM

Made in the USA
Middletown, DE
11 October 2023

40593198R00068